FLASHLIGHT

illustrated by Reina Rubel

FLASH·LIGHT

and other poems

by Judith Thurman

Atheneum · *1976* · *New York*

Library of Congress Cataloging in Publication Data
Thurman, Judith,
    Flashlight and other poems.
    SUMMARY: *A collection of poems reflecting some
of the major and minor encounters of childhood.*
    [1. American poetry]   I. Rubel, Reina.
II. Title.
PZ8.3.T42Fl   811'.5'4   75-29442
ISBN 0-689-30515-X

Copyright © 1976 by Judith Thurman
Published simultaneously in Canada by
McClelland & Stewart, Ltd.
Manufactured in the United States of America
Printed by The Murray Printing Company,
Forge Village, Massachusetts
Bound by H. Wolff, New York
First Edition

for Lilian Moore

CONTENTS

FLASHLIGHT

OIL SLICK

There, by the curb,
a leaky truck
has drooled
a grease-pool,

a black, pearly
slick
which rainbows
when the sun
strikes it.

I could spend
all day
marbling
its flashy colors
with a stick.

HYDRANT

The play-street
hydrant
gushes an icy
arc.

It makes
the gutter
into a rushing
river.

It makes
our brown, sticky,
summer bodies
shiver.

Even
its sound
is from some
mountain
ground.

LUMPS

Humps are lumps
and so are mumps.

Bumps make lumps
on heads.

Mushrooms grow
in clumps of lumps—
on clumps of stumps,
in woods and dumps.

Springs spring lumps
in beds.

Mosquito bites
make itchy lumps.

Frogs on logs
make twitchy lumps.

CAMPFIRE

We're sleeping in the woods.
We're strangers here.
The Milky Way
is thick as white breath
on the dark, cold air.

We eat and sing
and feed twigs to the fire:
bones it begs for,
leaping to lick our fingers.

FLASHLIGHT

My flashlight tugs me
through the dark
like a hound
with a yellow eye,

sniffs
at the edges
of steep places,

paws
at moles'
and rabbits'
holes,

points its nose
where sharp things
lie asleep—

and then it bounds
ahead of me
on home ground.

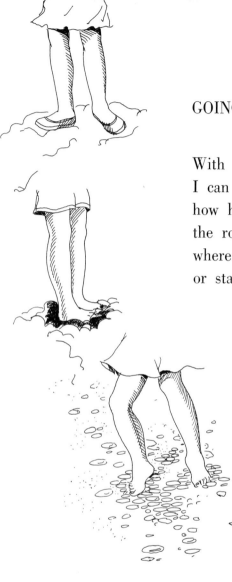

GOING BAREFOOT

With shoes on,
I can only feel
how hard or soft
the rock or sand is
where I walk
or stand.

Barefoot,
I can feel
how warm mud
molds my soles—
or how cold
pebbles
knead them
like worn knuckles.

Curling my toes,
I can drop
an anchor
to the sea floor—
hold fast
to the shore
when the tide
tows.

MARE

When the mare shows you
her yellow teeth, stuck
with clover and gnawed leaf,
you know they have combed
pastures of spiky grasses,
and tough thickets.

But when you offer her
a sweet, white lump
from the trembling plate
of your palm—she trots
to the gate, sniffs—
and takes it with velvet lips.

KISSES

Two
kisses for hello,
pressed like snaps
onto each cheek.

One
kiss for sleep-tight,
planted on the forehead
like a flag.

A handful
of kisses for good-bye,
wind-blown
like seeds or bubbles.

A spidery
kiss that tickles
a sad feeling.

TUNNEL

Tunnel coming!
I'm not afraid—
I plunge
through its
dark hoop,

feel-hear
its walls
rumble and hum,
as if I were
inside a drum.

Light!
I can see sun
piercing
the tight
drumskin.

I wish
I could keep
daybreak
in sight
that way—
all through
the night.

PRETENDING TO SLEEP

Pretending to sleep
in the back seat
I squeeze my eyelids
like the wings
of a caught moth.
They flutter—
but I breathe deep.

I suck my cheeks in
so I can't grin
when they whisper,
"We won't wake her."
I'm a good faker.

SPILL

the wind scatters
a flock of sparrows—
a handful of small change
spilled suddenly
from the cloud's pocket.

NEW NOTEBOOK

Lines
in a new notebook
run, even and fine,
like telephone wires
across a snowy landscape.

With wet, black strokes
the alphabet settles between them,
comfortable as a flock of crows.

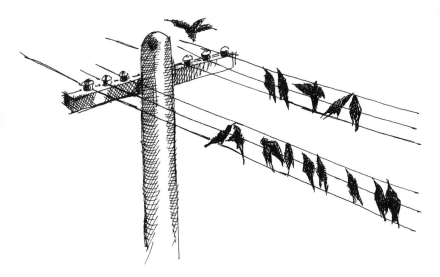

BALLOONS!

A balloon
is a wild
space animal,

restless pet
who bumps and butts
its head
on the cage walls
of a room—

bursts
with a bellow,
or escapes slowly
with sighs
leaving a limp skin.

Balloons
on the street
fidget
in fresh air,
strain
at their string
leashes.

If you loose
a balloon,
it bolts home
for the moon.

TURNING THE CORNER

With the wind at my back
I'm hustled home,
as if by a crowd behind me
in a revolving door.

With the wind against me,
the crowd's gone.
I push, push, PUSH
on that door, alone.

RAGS

The night wind
rips a cloud sheet
into rags,

then rubs, rubs
the October moon
until it shines
like a brass doorknob.

PLAYING WITH CLAY

Clay
is a clown
with no bones.

No roll,
stretch,
split—
no feat of change
is too great
for it.

Pinch
a thin nose,
a chin.

Gouge
two eye-holes.
Chisel
a grin.

Would you then
pummel him flat,
thumb him again?

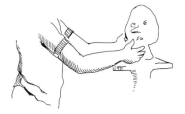

No!
He's become
someone.

BLIZZARD

The big city is rude to snow.
Trees shrug snow from their branches.
Sidewalks won't let snow stick.
Gutters refuse it too—
And so the snow melts into slush,
pretends that it never was.

Sometimes, though,
a snowfall captures the city,
sheets its statues,
tangles its streets.
Corners vanish: their policemen
whistle for them in vain.
Bus-bulls, tires spinning, snort and paw.
Even snowplows sniff at it—and stall.

A great snow hushes
the big sounds of the city.
Small sounds come out of hiding:
drops drumming on tin,
shovels strumming on narrow paths,
voices ringing in air
as clear as an empty glass.

City kids have wished all winter
for this morning.
They rush out,
hugging the snow with their bodies.

CLOSET

I like to
pretend

the raincoat
sleeves
are the leaves.

I like to
pretend

the slippery
boots
are the roots.

I like to
pretend

the old fur coat
is my friend,
the brown bear,

who lets me
hide
in her lair.

CLOCKFACE

Hours pass
slowly as a snail
creeping between the grassblades
of the minutes.

ZEBRA

white sun
black
fire escape,

morning
grazing like a zebra
outside my window.

ALMOST SPRING

One day in March
when the mud oozes,
rugs appear on windowsills
lolling like dusty tongues;
carts sell daffodils—
and the wind, like a paintbrush,
smacks my cheek freshly.

I take off my coat
and shoes, play
in the sun, sweat.
But in the shivery shade
it's not Spring, yet.

SKINNED KNEE

My knee
knits itself
with in-and-out
stitches,

a rough patch
that itches—
but don't scratch!

There's skin
below,
still soft,
still

whole.

SOAP

New cakes of soap
have names you can feel—
letters that stand up under fingers
like ears, lips, eyelids
on a soft face.

Old cakes of soap
are as smooth to stroke
as a chin.

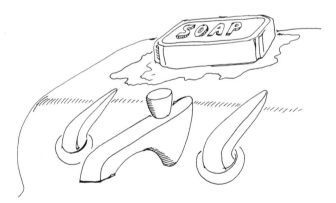

THE LITTLE RAIN

the little rain
writes its name
in the dust:
on hoods of cars.
on window panes.

The BIG rain
comes with a
s w o o s h:

    cars

      panes

        dust

          names

    w   h   o   o   s   h!

BREAKING THROUGH

Forks
of warm rain
loosen the ice
on the pond.

*

Morning
turns in the keyhole,
the dark gives,
it opens.

*

My seed
is growing.
A little shoot
has pushed through
the hard shell.